MAKING JEWELRY

by SHARON LERNER   pictures by GEORGE OVERLIE

Lerner Publications Company • Minneapolis, Minnesota

LIBRARY OF CONGRESS CATALOGING IN PUBLICATION DATA

Lerner, Sharon.
Making jewelry.

(An Early Craft Book)
SUMMARY: Instructions for using wire and sheet metal to make and decorate necklaces, rings, barrettes, earrings, and other jewelry.

1. Jewelry making — Juvenile literature. [1. Jewelry making. 2. Metalwork. 3. Handicraft] I. Overlie, George. II. Title.

TT212.L47   1977   745.59'42   76-13066
ISBN 0-8225-0862-1

International Standard Book Number: 0-8225-0862-1
Library of Congress Catalog Card Number: 76-13066

1 2 3 4 5 6 7 8 9 10 85 84 83 82 81 80 79 78 77

Contents

Why wear jewelry?

People wear shoes to protect their feet, and they wear clothes to cover their bodies. But why do people wear jewelry? Today many people wear jewelry just for fun. The word *jewelry* is, in fact, related to an ancient Latin word meaning "game" or "fun." But, in addition to being fun, jewelry can have many special meanings.

In ancient times, jewelry was a way of showing a person's status in life. In some ancient societies, unmarried women wore certain kinds of jewelry to let all potential husbands know that they were available. Married women wore other

kinds of jewelry to show their status. Even today, a gold or silver band on the "ring finger" tells the world that the wearer is married.

In tribal societies, the chief usually wore emblems of his office. A chief who was a great hunter probably wore the teeth or claws of a slain animal around his neck to show his bravery. In India, a wealthy man would often adorn his wife with jewels to show the world what a rich, important person he was. Today it is not unusual to see a wealthy or famous man wearing a diamond stickpin in his necktie. People even wore jewelry for sentimental reasons. Queen Victoria, for instance, kept a piece of her own baby hair in her locket, as do some people today.

Perhaps the importance of jewelry can best be shown by the fact that the ancient Egyptians and some Native Americans adorned their dead with beautiful pieces of jewelry for "life in the next world." Even today, people wear jewelry that symbolizes their spiritual lives—the cross is often worn by modern Christians, and the Star of David symbolizes the beliefs of its Jewish wearers.

Ancient and modern reasons for wearing jewelry are not so different after all. But the fact remains that modern jewelry is also "fun" apparel. The less expensive kind of "fun" jewelry is called *costume jewelry*. It is generally made from inexpensive metals, plastics, cork, or glass. Some jewelry makers can even create an attractive "primitive" look with the things that people in primitive societies actually used: bones, teeth, claws, shells, feathers, stones, seeds, and clay or glass beads. From these easy-to-find items, you, too, can make jewelry.

To begin work in jewelry making, you will learn to use metals as well as beads and shells. Though your jewelry will resemble primitive jewelry in its simplicity, it will be thoroughly modern, and it will be thoroughly "you." Your creation will, indeed, be an original that you can wear just for fun or for some special reason.

Tools for making wire jewelry

Jewelry made from pieces of bent and shaped wire is both easy to make and attractive. Most of the tools you need for working with wire are available at a hardware store or a hobby store. And many of the tools can be found around your own home. The first thing you should do before going to the store is to check the family tool cabinet for the things you need.

PLIERS A pliers is a tool used to shape, bend, and twist wire. Its jaws hold an item somewhat in the same way as the pincers of a tweezer do. You will need a small pliers of the smooth-jawed, flat, or round-nosed kind.

SNIPPERS OR NIPPERS These tools are used for cutting metal. If you have to buy a wire-cutting tool, get an "aircraft" snips, which is an excellent tool for cutting both sheet metal and wire.

SMALL METAL FILE A nail file will do nicely if you don't have a special file for metal.

HAMMER Any sturdy hammer will do; however, one with a ball end is really the best. You will use your hammer to *forge*, or shape and flatten, the wire.

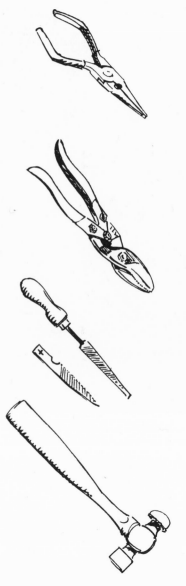

steel block

small anvil

vise with anvil

SMALL ANVIL An anvil is a metal "table" on which you flatten and shape your wire. The pressure of the hammer hitting the wire while it is lying on the anvil causes it to flatten. By hammering more on one part of a wire than on another, you can vary your shaping. If you have no anvil, the top part of a *vise*, or "holding" tool, can be used. Even a small, heavy block of metal works well.

FINE OR MEDIUM EMERY PAPER Both the file and the emery paper are used to smooth rough edges on metal. First use the file for the roughest edges, and then use the emery paper for finishing. You can also use sandpaper for finishing.

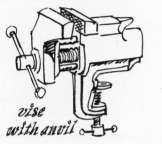

RULER OR TAPE MEASURE You will need one of these tools to measure lengths of wire.

Materials for making wire jewelry

Most jewelry makers use brass, copper, silver, or gold wire. But you may want to begin by experimenting on the less costly stovepipe, tin, or telephone wire. Once you have mastered a few jewelry-making techniques with inexpensive wire, you may want to use the better copper or brass wire. And when you have made many fine pieces from copper or brass, you may want to try silver. Gold, because it is very expensive, should be left to very experienced jewelry makers. The wire you need for making jewelry can be bought at a craft supply store or a hardware store.

STOVEPIPE OR TIN WIRE Buy about five feet (1.5 meters) of this "practice" wire so that you can get the "feel" for shaping wire. After practicing with inexpensive stovepipe or tin wire, you will be ready to work on brass or copper wire.

stovepipe wire

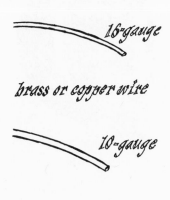

16-gauge

brass or copper wire

10-gauge

SOFT BRASS OR COPPER WIRE You will need about 25 feet (7.5 meters) of 14- to 16-gauge wire. The gauge of a wire tells you its thickness. The higher the number is, the thinner the wire will be. For example, a 16-gauge wire is thinner than a 10-gauge wire. "Soft" wire is the best wire for the decorative part of the necklace, and "half-hard" wire is the best wire for a neck ring.

AN ASSORTMENT OF BEADS Look for discarded bracelets and necklaces to cut apart. Choose the most interesting beads from these, or buy beads of wood, plastic, glass, or bone. Beads can be bought singly, in bags, or on strings at a craft supply store or at a yarn and needlework shop. You will probably have fun looking for beads of different sizes and shapes. But, as you are doing so, be sure that the *eyes*, or holes, in the beads you choose are big enough for a wire, a leather lace, or a cord to pass through.

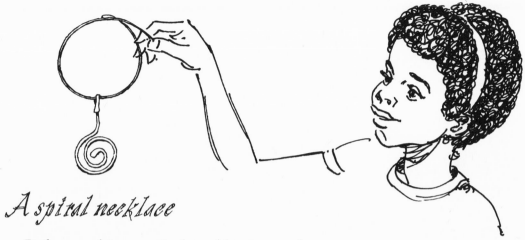

A spiral necklace

Before making a spiral necklace out of copper or brass wire, practice making a spiral out of stovepipe wire. Begin by snipping about nine inches (22.5 centimeters) of wire from your roll. To make the spiral, shape one end of the wire into a small curl with your pliers. Following the curve of the curl, shape the wire so that it bends in two more curls, each larger than the one before it. At first, your spiral may have kinks and clumsy-looking bends, but it will look more graceful as you practice.

When you feel "at home" shaping stovepipe

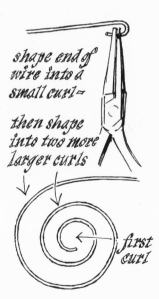

shape end of wire into a small curl ~

then shape into two more larger curls

first curl

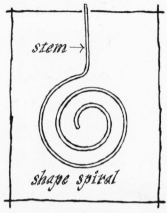

stem →

shape spiral

forge spiral

pound both ends flat

wire, snip off nine inches of brass or copper wire. Make a spiral with it and bend the wire up at the outside end to form a stem about an inch long. How does your spiral look? Gently adjust it so that it looks good to you.

Now put your spiral on the anvil and *forge*, or pound, it with a hammer to flatten the wire slightly. By forging the metal, you are "locking in" the design you want. Forging also makes your wire look more interesting, because the flattened surfaces show texture and pick up light better. Be sure to pound both ends very flat so that they look like little canoe paddles. Use the ball of your hammer to pound the end inside the spiral. Then use your file to smooth the flattened ends. File back and forth over the edges to make them smooth and round.

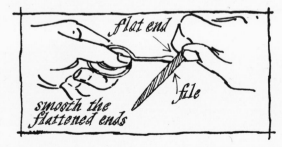

flat end

file

smooth the flattened ends

form loop on stem

pliers

14

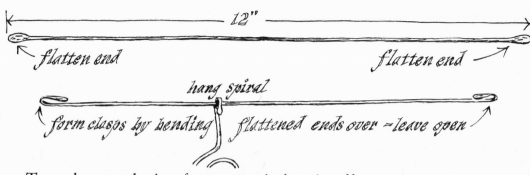

12"

flatten end   *flatten end*

hang spiral

form clasps by bending flattened ends over ~ leave open

To make a neck ring for your spiral, snip off about 12 inches (30 centimeters) of "half-hard" wire (or less if you have a very small neck). Forge each end, canoe-paddle style, and file the ends until they are round and smooth. Now hang the spiral on the neck ring.

To form the clasps of the neck ring, use your pliers to bend each end of the neck ring over about three-quarters of an inch (about two centimeters). Do not pinch these new bends together. Instead, shape the neck ring in a circle and hook the bent ends together to fasten the necklace. If you would rather not wear a neck ring, you can hang your spiral from a leather lace or a cord. To fasten this kind of necklace, simply tie the ends in a knot at the back of your neck.

shape neck ring into a circle

knot

cord or leather thong

A spiral necklace with beads

The wire spiral can be used in a variety of necklaces. For example, it can be combined with smaller spirals and beads for a more elaborate look. You may want to try the following necklace, which has three spirals and four beads.

First snip off one nine-inch (22.5-centimeter) length of wire and two six-inch (15-centimeter) pieces of wire. Bend the wire pieces into three spirals, one large spiral and two small ones. Forge the spirals and their ends as you did before. File the ends so that they look and feel smooth.

With a pliers, bend the stems of the large

1.
cut 3 pieces
of wire
9″
6″

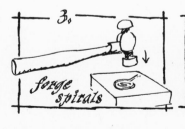

2.
bend wire pieces
into a spiral

3.
forge
spirals

4.
file smooth

spiral and one of the small spirals into loops. Then turn over the remaining small spiral and make a loop in it. (By turning one spiral over to make the loop, you are making sure that the small spirals will face opposite directions on the neck ring.) Tighten all the loops.

Now snip off a neck-ring wire and shape it. Hang the large spiral in the middle of the ring and place one bead on either side of the spiral. Then hang the small spirals, one on the outside of each bead. Add two more beads, one next to each small spiral. You can vary this design by adding more beads between the spirals or by adding different colors and kinds of beads. When you finally decide on an arrangement, finish the ends of the neck ring, and clasp them together to form a circle.

6.

snip off neck-ring wire ~ shape

ends unfinished

hang large spiral

add one bead each side

add small spirals and other two beads

finish neck ring ends clasp together

5.

form loop on large spiral

form loop on small spirals

turn over

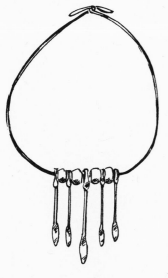

A wire-toothed necklace with beads

Another attractive necklace can be made from shorter lengths of wire, some beads, and a cord or a neck ring. To begin, snip off one two-inch (five-centimeter) piece of wire and four one-and-a-half-inch (about four-centimeter) pieces of wire. These will be the "teeth" of your necklace.

Forge each piece of wire. Work especially hard on all the ends to flatten them. (Each piece should look like a little canoe paddle, with one end more rounded than the other.) Then file the ends until they look and feel smooth. Bend the smaller end of each piece into a tight loop.

If you use a cord or a lace, be sure to choose beads with large holes. Begin stringing by centering the longest "tooth" on the cord.

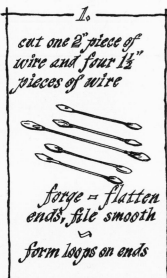

1.

cut one 2" piece of wire and four 1½" pieces of wire

forge = flatten ends, file smooth

form loops on ends

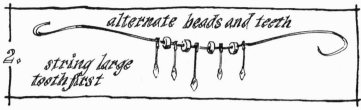

2. string large tooth first · alternate beads and teeth

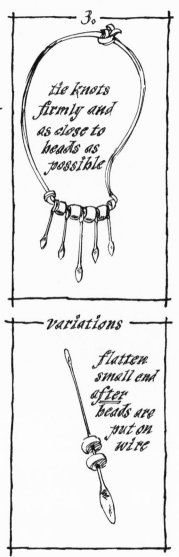

3. tie knots firmly and as close to beads as possible

— *variations* —

flatten small end *after* beads are put on wire

String a bead on each side of it. Then, working in both directions on the cord, add a shorter tooth and a bead. When you have strung the final teeth and beads, make sure that your arrangement is centered on the cord. Then tie firm knots as close as possible to the outer beads. These knots will secure your design on the cord.

There are many variations on this design. You can, for example, put a bead on the middle tooth; just remember to forge the loop end of the tooth only *after* the bead is on. Or you may want to use three teeth instead of five.

These are only a few ideas for wire and bead necklaces. Once you have become familiar with working in wire, you will see that there are endless possibilities for new and exciting designs.

A wire ring

Rings have long been a popular form of jewelry. Perhaps they are popular because they are ornaments that people can see themselves wearing. People need only glance at their hands to notice the effect of rings.

Today rings are very fashionable, especially when several are worn on one hand. On the following pages, the techniques for making one basic wire ring will be described. Once you learn how to make it, you can create a whole collection of different rings for yourself.

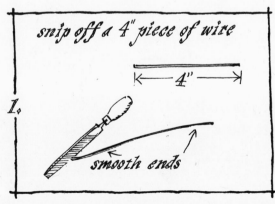

1. *snip off a 4" piece of wire*

← 4" →

smooth ends

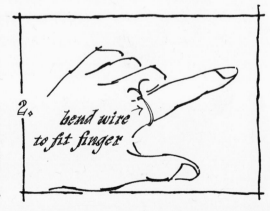

2. *bend wire to fit finger*

To make a ring, snip off a four-inch (10-centimeter) piece of wire. With a file and some emery paper, smooth both ends of the wire. Beginning at the middle, bend the wire to form a circle that will fit your finger. Then, with the pliers, bend two small spirals, one at each end of the wire. Forge the spirals until they are flat, and adjust the wire so that the spirals come close together to form the top of the ring. You can vary this design by adding a bead to each end of the wire before forming the spirals and forging them. How does your ring look and feel? If necessary, you can re-adjust the wire for a better fit.

A variation

add beads before forming spirals

3. form 2 small spirals

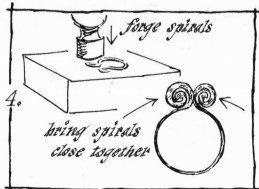

4. forge spirals

bring spirals close together

A barrette and pick

To hold long, thick hair, a pick barrette (buh-REHT) is just the thing. The forged metal will highlight your hair as well as hold it in place.

To make the barrette, snip off a 14-inch (35-centimeter) piece of wire. With the pliers, bend a small spiral at each end. Bend the rest of the wire back and forth in a wavy design. Each "wave" should be about an inch and a half (3.75 centimeters) long. Pound the entire barrette until it is flat, and flatten the ends even

1.

one 14" long piece of wire

bend small spiral in each end

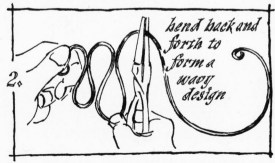

2.

bend back and forth to form a wavy design

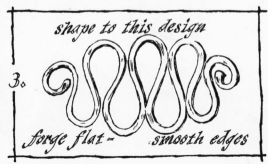

3.

shape to this design

forge flat — smooth edges

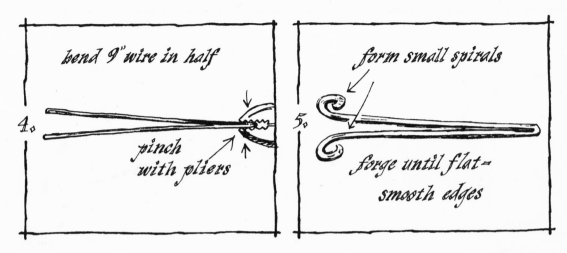

4. bend 9" wire in half

pinch
with pliers

5. form small spirals

forge until flat—
smooth edges

more. File them so that they are smooth and round.

To make the pick that will hold the barrette in place, snip off a nine-inch (22.5-centimeter) piece of wire. File the ends until they are smooth. Then bend the wire in half. With the pliers, pinch the wire as tightly as you can at its bend, which will become the "point" of the pick. Then make a small spiral at each end of the wire, and forge the entire pick until it is flat. To wear the barrette, lay it on top of your hair and push the pick into one spiral, under the hair, and out through the other spiral.

Sheet-metal jewelry

Another very attractive kind of jewelry is made from brass, copper, or silver sheet metal. Sheet metal, unfortunately, can be rather expensive. It is also hard to find at times, and it can be difficult to cut. For your purposes, tin-can covers are a good substitute for sheet metal: they are easy to obtain and easy to cut with a snips. The major problem with tin-can covers, however, is that they have jagged edges. But, with extra caution, you can make attractive and unusual jewelry without hurting yourself.

In addition to the tools you used for making wire jewelry, you will need a two-inch (five-

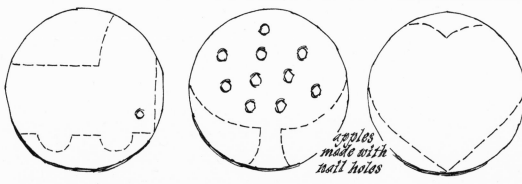

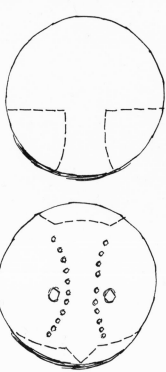

apples made with nail holes

centimeter) nail and a small, thick block of wood. You will use these two tools for punching holes in your jewelry. The holes will be needed for hanging pieces from a cord, for attaching two pieces with wire, or simply for decorating jewelry.

Pendants made out of the lids of juice cans are easy to design. All you have to do to create designs is to sketch a few ideas first. Do this by tracing half a dozen can-lid circles on paper. Then "play" with designs that will fit in the circles. You can draw a mushroom, perhaps, or a turtle, a heart, a flower, an owl, or a leaf. All of these designs have curves that can be made to fit the curve of a can lid.

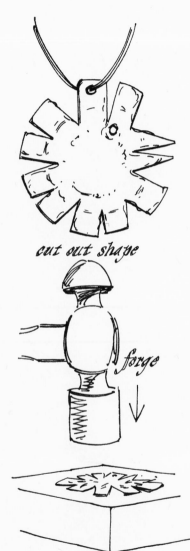

cut out shape

forge

← metal anvil

A sunfish pendant

Suppose you decide to make a sunfish for your first pendant. A proper sunfish has three top fins, three bottom fins, a tail and a mouth. To form these parts, use your snips to cut eight small triangles in the juice-can lid. Where the face of the fish is to be, make the triangles a little larger, leaving a rectangular piece between them for the lips of the fish. Always work carefully with can lids, because the jagged metal edges are sharp.

Place the fish disk on your anvil and forge the edges and the surface. If the cover is embossed with print, forge it out. A few swift hits will flatten the words and give the metal an interesting texture. Forging will also flatten the sharp edges and give them a natural, more irregular look.

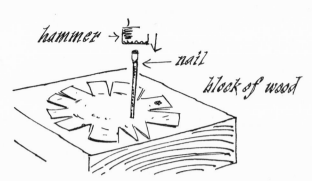

hammer → nail ← block of wood

file all sharp edges carefully finish with emery paper

knot

knot

Now place your fish on the block of wood. With the hammer and nail, pound two holes in the fish, one for the eye and one to string the neck cord through. Carefully file and sand the back of each hole until all the sharp edges are gone. File and sand all the edges, too, until they look and feel smooth. To get into the inner points of the triangles, use an emery board or a small nail file. Take the time to do a thorough job of filing and sanding.

You are now ready to slip a cord through the top hole in the pendant and wear it. To keep the pendant from slipping around on the cord, find the cord's center and tie a knot in it just above the hole. Tie the ends of the cord together to fasten the pendant around your neck.

A triangular pendant with beads

Any pendant shape that you think of can be easily combined with other similar shapes to make a more elaborate necklace. These shapes can be linked together with pieces of wire. You can also add beads to your design. A soup-can cover will provide enough metal for the triangle part of the necklace, and some beads and wire will add the finishing touches.

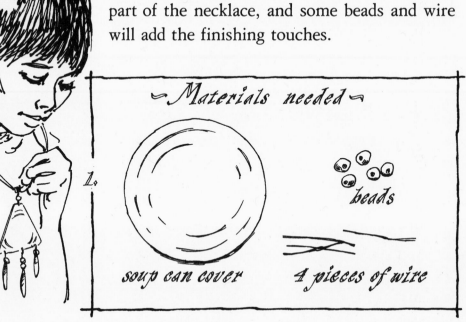

~ *Materials needed* ~

1.

soup can cover

beads

4 pieces of wire

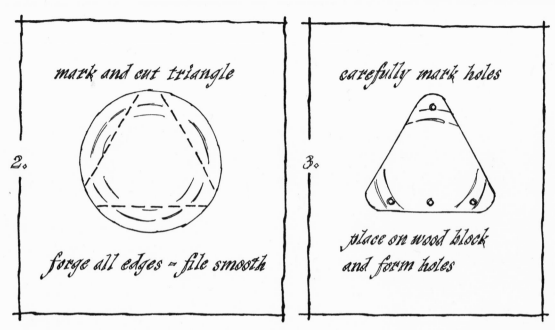

2.

mark and cut triangle

forge all edges ~ file smooth

3.

carefully mark holes

place on wood block and form holes

The soup-can top you choose may have a set of circles around its edge. Instead of forging them out, use these lines as part of your design. Cut away three "sides" of the circle to make a triangle. Then forge the edges and the surface of the triangle until you are pleased with its appearance.

Place the triangle on your block of wood, and pound one hole in the top and three along the

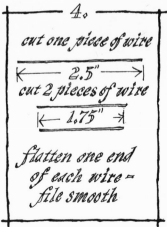

4.

cut one piece of wire

|← 2.5" →|

cut 2 pieces of wire

|← 1.75" →|

flatten one end of each wire ~ file smooth

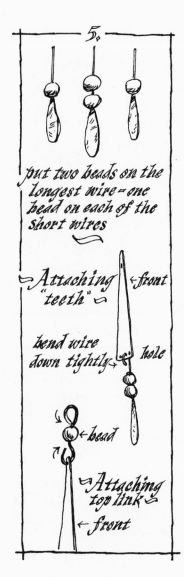

put two beads on the longest wire — one bead on each of the short wires

Attaching "teeth" → front

bend wire down tightly → hole

← bead

Attaching top link

← front

bottom. Make the three holes so that they are spaced evenly along the bottom edge. Carefully file and sand all the edges and the backs of the holes.

Now cut three pieces of wire, two 1.75 inches (4.5 centimeters) long and one 2.5 inches (6.25 centimeters) long. Forge the ends of the wires flat, canoe-paddle style, and file them to round off the rough edges.

Put two beads on the longest wire. Then, going from front to back, put a fourth of an inch of the wire into the middle bottom hole. Using a pliers, bend the short end of the wire down tightly against the back of the triangle to make a link. Add beads to the other two wires and attach them to the triangle in the same way.

To make a link for the top hole, cut 1.5 inches (3.75 centimeters) of wire, put it in the hole, and bend it up. Put a bead on it, and bend the rest of the wire down to complete the link. You are now ready to hang your pendant on a cord.

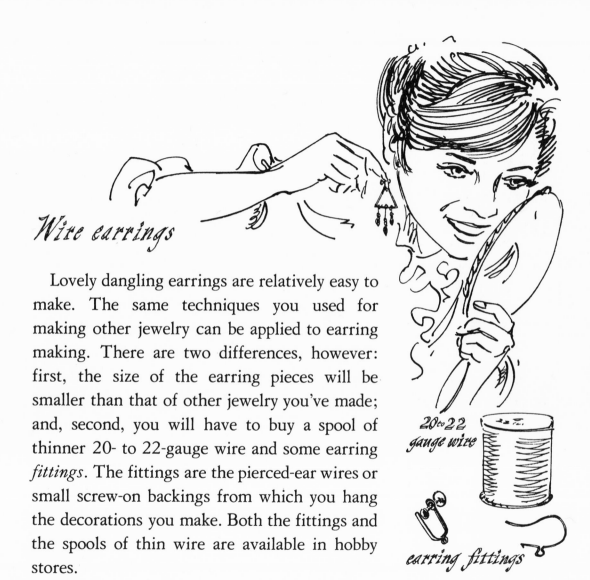

Wire earrings

Lovely dangling earrings are relatively easy to make. The same techniques you used for making other jewelry can be applied to earring making. There are two differences, however: first, the size of the earring pieces will be smaller than that of other jewelry you've made; and, second, you will have to buy a spool of thinner 20- to 22-gauge wire and some earring *fittings*. The fittings are the pierced-ear wires or small screw-on backings from which you hang the decorations you make. Both the fittings and the spools of thin wire are available in hobby stores.

20 to 22 gauge wire

earring fittings

You may want to try a pair of spiral earrings first. Or you may want metal "teeth" on your earrings instead. Forge short pieces of wire as before, and hang them singly or with beads on the earring fittings. You can also cut and shape small triangles or circles to hang with tiny seed beads from earring fittings.

After all the work you have put into making necklaces, rings, and earrings, you can see that jewelry is more than just "fun" apparel. Whatever your reason for making and wearing jewelry, you will probably feel a great satisfaction at wearing something you have created yourself. And the lasting beauty you create in metal will please your friends and relatives as well. They will enjoy wearing "originals" handcrafted especially for them, and you will enjoy creating and giving these special gifts.